I0707479

Keto Diet Pocket Guide

Benefits, Symptoms, Natural Remedies, Foods, Facts, and 4 of the Best Keto Recipes and Shopping List.

By Derek Shawn

Disclaimer

Copyright 2018 Derek Shawn

The information in this book cannot be used to diagnose or treat patients. The information and opinions have been simplified. Readers should not rely on this information as a substitute for a professional opinion.

FDA Compliance: The information in this book has not been evaluated by the Food & Drug Administration or any other medical body. We do not aim to diagnose, treat, cure, or prevent any illness or disease. Information is shared for educational purposes only. You must consult your doctor before acting on any content in this book, especially if you are pregnant, nursing, or taking medication, or if you have a medical condition.

This publication can be printed by the purchaser, for use by the purchaser only. Otherwise, no part of this publication may be reproduced or transmitted in any form or by any means, electronic or mechanical, including photocopying, recording or by any information storage and retrieval system, without written permission from the author, except as permitted by U.S. copyright law.

There are no representations or warranties, express or implied, about the completeness, accuracy, reliability, suitability, or availability with respect to the information, products, or services contained in this publication for any purpose. The author does not assume and hereby disclaims any liability to any party for any loss, damage, or disruption caused by errors or omissions. Any use of this information is at your own risk. The methods described in this publication are the author's personal thoughts. They are not intended to be a definitive set of instructions. You may discover that there are other methods to accomplish the same end result. If you wish to apply ideas contained in this publication, you are taking full responsibility for your actions. This information does not take the place of advice from your doctor. This is not an exhaustive treatment of the subjects. You are responsible for your own choices, actions, and results. Never disregard professional medical advice or delay seeking medical treatment because of something you have read in this book. The author is not a doctor and does not recommend, endorse, or make any representation about the efficacy, appropriateness, or suitability of any specific tests, products, procedures, treatments, services, opinions, health care providers, or other information in this book. Consult your doctor before changing your diet or medications. The keto diet is not recommended when pregnant or breastfeeding. The author is not responsible for any advice, course of treatment, or diagnosis that is obtained through this book. If you think you have a medical emergency, call your doctor, go to the emergency room, or call 911 immediately.

Contents

Introduction

The ketogenic diet (KD) is being practiced everywhere, and numerous people are achieving amazing results! The KD has been found to be incredibly beneficial for many illnesses. Though this way of life has become most popular only in recent years, the actual diet in its most current form was developed nearly 100 years ago in the 1920's, as a cure for epilepsy. As medications for epilepsy were developed, the KD lost ground (Freeman JM 2007). Over the years, the diet has regained traction; it is now known as a high-fat, low-carb diet that produces many health benefits, most notably easy weight loss (Volek J.S. 2009).

The KD is a high-fat, low-carb, and moderate protein diet. It's hard for some to imagine that a high-fat diet could contribute to weight loss, but numerous studies show that this is the case. When your body uses up all its glucose, it is forced to turn fat into ketones to use as energy. This process is known as ketosis, or "Nutritional Ketosis" (NK).

Many are choosing good health and achieving results with the ketogenic diet. People who have been fighting obesity for years are now winning this battle. This is having a tremendous impact and changing lives. However, this undertaking is not always an easy one. Side effects are causing people

to drop out before they see results. Food addictions
are causing people to stray. Knowledge can be like a
bridge spanning failure and success. A lack of
knowledge about how to cope is a significant hurdle.
This book will provide information and tools that
will empower you, including:

-Benefits of the keto diet
-A complete list of keto foods
-A list of side effects and natural remedies
-Tips for eating keto
-Types of keto diets
-Supplements
-The 4 best keto dishes, ever
-A grocery shopping list

Remember to listen to your hunger; cravings
tell you what foods you need. However, do not heed
your food addictions. Processed sugar, refined
grains, and processed carbs are not generally
considered nutritious, so if you are craving these,
you may have an addiction rather than a nutritional
deficiency. As the famous Hypocrites said: "Let food
be thy medicine and medicine be thy food."

The body's ability to adapt is remarkable.
Since prehistoric times the human race has had to
conform to its environment. The change in seasons
has required people to scavenge for meat and

anything they could find during the winter months and through the ice ages. It's not a coincidence that meats and other foods high in fat provide more energy and sustenance than fruits and vegetables do. People would have needed this long-lasting, high-energy food source to keep themselves warm and alive while they attempted to survive in cold climates. Just think of the foods that would have been available to our ancestors living in a frozen landscape.

Our bodies get used to eating a certain way. When we change the way we eat, our bodies must adapt. People can experience a range of symptoms when they change their diets. Eat a large salad when you haven't had one in a while. Eat a jalapeno cheeseburger after you've been eating a vegetarian diet for the last year. You will most likely be running for the bathroom. Sudden and drastic diet changes can be hard on your body. The slower you make those changes to your diet, the more easily your body will adapt.

How easy will it be for you to start seeing results? It may be harder if you have medical issues, are on medications, or are overweight. It may be easier if you are healthy, practice fasting, or already eat similar foods. It's up to you to find success. However, you shouldn't have to suffer to achieve results. If you have concerns or feel that something is not right, see a doctor; don't risk your wellbeing. Not everyone has a hard time with this diet. That's one reason why the KD is popular. People are making progress, and it's easy.

Part 1
Benefits of the Keto Diet!

Look at these commonly reported benefits, backed by legitimate scientific research. See the back of this book for more information about citations, research, and studies.

1. Weight loss

People who have been trying to lose weight for years are finding success in nutritional ketosis. Low-carb diets have been shown to contribute to weight loss more than low-fat diets do (Volek J.S. 2009).

The obesity rate among adult Americans has been estimated at 32.2% for men and 35.5% for women (Katherine M. Flegal 2010). Obesity is an epidemic and has been linked to a variety of health conditions, including type 2 diabetes, high blood pressure, heart disease, strokes, certain types of cancer, sleep apnea, osteoarthritis, fatty liver disease, kidney disease, and pregnancy problems, to name just a few (Pi-Sunyer 2009).

As you can see, maintaining an ideal weight can do amazing things for your health. Some of us know how much better a person feels when he or she is at an optimal weight.

2. Type 2 diabetes

The keto diet has also been shown to improve blood-sugar levels and decrease the need for insulin (Yancy 2005). People have reported that NK reversed and even cured their diabetes. If you include exercise with your diet regimen, you may see better results. Exercise can significantly improve health, especially when it's coupled with diet. The transformation can be incredible.

3. Epilepsy

For years, the KD has been a primary treatment for epilepsy. It has been proven to decrease seizures, even after the patient transitioned off NK (Martin K 2016). This was the primary use for keto when it was developed in the 1920's.

4. Cardiovascular disease

Based on the available literature, the KD is associated with improvements in cardiovascular risk factors, such as obesity, type 2 diabetes, and HDL cholesterol levels (Kosinski 2017). This is great news for your cardiovascular health.

5. Metabolic syndrome

Metabolic syndrome is quite common. Approximately 32 percent of the population in the U.S. has metabolic syndrome, and about 85 percent of those with type 2 diabetes have metabolic syndrome. Metabolic syndrome is characterized by a combination of several symptoms, including high blood pressure, high blood sugar, abdominal weight gain, and high cholesterol (Ford ES 2010). Carbohydrate restriction has a more favorable impact on the metabolic syndrome than does a low-fat diet (Volek J.S. 2009). Low-carb diets have been shown to decrease blood pressure, lower blood sugar, boost weight loss, and improve cholesterol levels – potentially reducing your risk of heart disease, stroke, and diabetes (Staff 2017). In one small study, all 22 subjects were cured of metabolic syndrome within 12 weeks while they were on the "Spanish Ketogenic Mediterranean diet" (Pérez-Guisado J1 2011). This is a massive win for keto diets!

6. Polycystic ovarian syndrome

This condition affects women. Symptoms include irregular or no menstrual periods, heavy periods, excess body and facial hair, acne, pelvic pain, difficulty getting pregnant, and patches of thick, dark, velvety skin (Gynecologists 2015). Associated conditions include type 2 diabetes, obesity, obstructive sleep apnea, heart disease, mood disorders, and endometrial cancer (other 2017). The study suggests that people with PCOS who transition to a low-carb or keto diet make significant improvements (Mavropoulos 2005).

7. Irritable bowel syndrome

Low-carb and keto diets have been reported to improve or even eliminate IBS. Many in the medical industry say that IBS has no cure and that those with this condition must simply manage the symptoms, but studies show that these medial experts may be wrong (Austin 2009).

8. Cholesterol

The ketogenic diet has been shown to raise HDL (good) cholesterol and lower LDL (bad) cholesterol (Dashti HM1 2004).

9. Other reported benefits

-Reduced inflammation (Masino 2013).
-Improved stress management (Brownlow 2017)
-Decreased headaches, fatigue, and depression (Di Lorenzo 2018)
-Improvements in anxiety, depression, bipolar disorder, schizophrenia, autism spectrum disorder

(ASD), and attention deficit hyperactivity disorder
(ADHD) (Bostock 2017)
-Improvements in certain types of cancers and
neurological diseases (Allen 2014)

Part 2
Symptoms and Remedies

People experience a range of symptoms while transitioning to the keto diet. Some of these symptoms may be caused by the foods one is consuming, while other symptoms may be caused by the transitioning process. Keep in mind that no one experiences all these symptoms, and many people don't experience any symptoms whatsoever. That being said, here's a helpful list of potential symptoms and natural remedies.

Always consult a doctor for health issues or before you change your diet/medications or take supplements.

1. Bad breath: The KD can cause higher acidity in the body. Lemon juice is a good natural remedy for bad breath; it kills bacteria and freshens your breath.

2. Confusion, anxiety, irritability and general withdrawal symptoms. Meditation and natural sedatives may help. This will pass with time. A clear mental state is most common while in NK.

3. Constipation: Natural remedies include adequate water, sodium, potassium, magnesium, and laxatives.

4. Dehydration/excessive thirst. The water in raw fruits and vegetables hydrates better than plain water. Drinking plenty of water is vital. Adequate sodium intake also helps tremendously.

5. Depression: Get some sunshine. The link between depressive disorders and Vitamin D deficiency from a lack of sun exposure is well-established and was first noted 2,000 years ago (C.C. 2012). Vegetables, berries, mushrooms, tomatoes, and nuts are also good foods for lifting your spirit.

6. Diarrhea: Eat more solid foods. Drink plenty of water and broth to replenish electrolytes. Avoid nuts, dairy, spicy foods, fried foods, and prepackaged foods.

7. Diminished physical performance/fatigue. Drink water, do some light exercises/increase your physical activity, and eat more carbs.

8. Leg cramps: Consume magnesium, potassium, sodium, water, electrolytes, and carbohydrates.

9. Fatty liver/liver pain. People have reported relief using liver supplements and natural herbs. Talk to a doctor if you are experiencing pain.

10. Frequent urination. Try to hold it. You can actually train your bladder to last longer between urinations. Some natural foods are also reported to help. These include cranberries, fenugreek seed, spinach, sesame seeds, and aloe vera juice.

11. Gallstones. Some have reported issues with gallstones on the keto diet. Potential natural remedies include a liver flush, a gallbladder flush, and other gallstone breakup products/herbs (like stonebreaker). People have reported much success with these products and natural herbs.

12. Hair loss. In time, your hair may grow in thicker than it was previously. Natural hair loss remedies include B-vitamins and Zinc. Minoxidil works for two out of three men. Finasteride slows or stops hair loss 90 percent of the time.

13. Hunger. You are probably going to want to eat everything you're not supposed to eat.

Your body has been conditioned to eat in a certain way. Many cells in your body and microorganisms in your gut will protest, but it will pass. Eat foods that you are craving and that go with your regimen.

14. Insomnia. Traditional herbs like passionflower, valerian, lavender, St John's wort, and chamomile help. Melatonin is a supplement that works well; it is the naturally occurring hormone in the body that causes you to sleep.

15. Keto rash. This is a rash caused by ketosis, which is more common when one is fasting. It will generally go away within a week or two. Some cases will require changes to one's diet to see improvement (Jason D. Michaels M.D. 2015).

16. Keto/carb flu. *See below.

17. Kidney stones. Ketones cause higher urine acidity and contribute to a higher risk of kidney stones. This was more common when the diet was introduced in the 1920's because fluid restriction was originally a part of the KD (Kossoff EH 2009).

18. Menstrual cramps/worse menstrual cycles. Common advice is to eat more carbs or eat more food in general.

19. Muscle loss. Some people have reported the loss of lean muscle mass along with their fat loss. You need more carbs, protein, and/or calories. Be careful, though; too much protein or too many carbs can take you out of ketosis.

20. Tachycardia, heart rhythm disorder (arrhythmia). Natural remedies include increasing consumption of whole organic, unprocessed foods and green vegetables, as well as decreasing consumption of processed foods, foods with hormones, and foods with pesticides. The body's use of ketones may contribute to a higher risk of arrhythmia (Best TH 2000).

"The Keto (Carb) Flu"

The keto flu feels like being sick. You could experience:
-Vomiting
-Shakes
-Cold sweating and chills
-Stomachache

-Poor sleep
-Withdrawal symptoms from changing diet
-Dizziness

Chicken broth/bone broth, electrolytes, and increased sodium intake can help tremendously. Increasing your carbs will also help. Don't forget to get a good night's sleep.

Common keto remedies

The following foods help with the transition to the KD: bone broth, chicken broth, salt/sodium, water, vegetables, nuts, increased carbs, starches, and green smoothies (made with vegetables).

Keto Supplements

Recommended dietary allowances:
Magnesium: 420 mg or less per day depending on age
Potassium: 4,700 mg per day for adults. *Potassium overdose can be fatal
Sodium: 2300 mg per day
Calcium: 1,300 mg per day
Vitamin D (unless you get enough sun)
Probiotics: sauerkraut, yogurt, kefir
Fish oil: found to optimize triglyceride levels while one is on the KD (Meidenbauer JJ 2014)

*Additional amounts of certain supplements may help when one is on the KD.
*Consult your doctor before taking supplements.
*Remember: Supplements aren't always as good a source of vitamins and minerals as actual foods. Sometimes, the body absorbs only a small percentage of the supplement.

Part 3
Keto Foods

You can eat many foods on the ketogenic diet. You can even convert your existing diet into one of a keto variety. If you're on the paleo diet, or a vegetarian or vegan diet, keto can still work for you. You have choices. You can incorporate plant-based fats or animal fats. You can eat processed foods, or you can eat whole foods. The different food choices you make will have a considerable effect on your success and the way you feel.

I've put together a list of whole foods commonly eaten on the KD. This can serve as a reference when you have questions about what to eat. Check the ingredients and nutrients on packaged foods and track your protein, carbs, and caloric intake. Use a nutrition app on your phone or computer to track your "macros" (i.e., macronutrients: fats, proteins, carbs, and calories).

Here's what you can eat:

Veggies:

Salad greens, kale, cabbage, arugula, parsley, cilantro, basil, broccoli, cauliflower, zucchini, squash, pumpkin, turnips, celery, rhubarb, radishes, mushrooms, onions (in moderation), chives, garlic, bell peppers (in moderation), jalapeños (in moderation), artichokes, brussels sprouts, asparagus, green beans, and eggplant

Proteins:

Chicken, turkey, pork, beef, tofu, tempeh, some veggie burgers, salmon, tuna, whitefish, crab, clams, mussels, oysters, eggs, and sardines

*All meats are good for NK. I try to stick to organic, unprocessed, fresh, hormone-free meats and grass-fed beef.

Whole grains/flours:

Almond flour, coconut flour, and Bob's Red Mill Low-Carb Baking Mix

Noodles:

Shirataki noodles, black bean pasta, almond flour pasta, and some types of egg pasta/homemade egg pasta

Fruits:

Lemon, tomatoes, cucumbers, watermelon (in moderation), blueberries, blackberries, raspberries, cranberries, and strawberries (berries in moderation)

Healthy fats/dairy:

Butter, sour cream, heavy whipping cream, yogurt, kefir, ghee, cottage cheese, cheese, avocado, olive oil, coconut oil, seeds, nuts and nut butters, flax seeds, mayonnaise, dark chocolate, and cocoa powder

Snacks:

Pork rinds, seaweed, "fat bombs," veggie sticks, "keto cookies," nuts, sardines, pickles, jerky, string cheese, dark chocolate, and "keto bread"; look for additional low-carb and keto-friendly products at your local grocery store.

Low-carb sugar substitutes:

Monkfruit, stevia, erythritol, and "sukrin" sweeteners; some of these products may have side effects.

Healing foods:

Vegetables, nuts, bone broth, chicken broth, and green smoothies (made with vegetables); please note: If you are not feeling well, increasing your carb, salt/sodium, and water intake can sometimes make you feel better when you are having difficulties while on the KD.

Foods to stay away from:

Sugar, grains, starchy vegetables, vegetables that grow underground, potatoes, noodles, bread, grains, pop, juice, fruits, raisins, cranberry sauce, pizza, energy bars, beer, candy, donuts, margarine, foods with trans fats, and processed foods.

Inducing/maintaining ketosis:

Keep your carbohydrates under 20g day, for 1-4 days, to induce ketosis. Most people will want to keep their carbs between <20-80g per day to maintain a state of ketosis (after inducing ketosis). Always test your urine for ketones to ensure success. Ketosis is dependent on many factors, including age, weight, physical activity levels, and types of fats/foods consumed.

Keto diet guidelines:

Protein: 20%-30%: 0.7-1 gram of protein per pound of body weight, daily. If you work out you will want to consume 1-1.2 grams of protein per pound of body weight, daily. Protein has approximately 4 calories per gram.

Fat: 50%-75% of calories from high fats and oils. This equals 1,000-1,500 calories from fat when one is on a 2,000-calorie diet. Fats have approximately 9 calories per gram.

Carbs: 5%-10%. Try to find your optimum level. Carbs have approximately 4 calories per gram.

The 4 Best Keto Dishes, Ever

Eating while on the KD doesn't have to be complicated. Add a high fat side dish or "fat bomb" to these meals to lower your overall carbohydrate ratio. Nutritional information and cook times are approximate. Here are some great-tasting meals anyone can make. These meals have good proportions to help keep you in NK!

You should see pictures of these meals! Visit our Facebook page at: www.facebook.com/Keto-diet-pocket-guidebook-406647719847530 Like our Facebook page to receive recipes and free offers!

#1. Keto Spaghetti

Nutrition facts
Servings per meal: 4
Time to cook: 25 minutes
Calories: 379
Fat: 26 grams (234 calories from fat = 62% of meal)
Protein: 24 grams (96 calories from protein = 25% of meal)
Carbs: 14 grams (56 calories from carbs = 15% of meal)
Add a fat bomb side dish to this meal to improve macro ratios.

Ingredients:

1 ½ cups mushrooms, sliced
1 small can olives, sliced
1 cup chopped tomatoes
2 cloves garlic, finely minced
1 pound organic grass-fed ground beef, 80% (20% fat)
½ teaspoon salt
2 tablespoons Italian seasoning
1 can (24 oz) Hunts garlic and herb pasta sauce
2 tablespoons parmesan cheese
2 packages low-carb pasta "spaghetti - skinny pasta" (konjac/shirataki noodles)

*Please note: You can use several other types of low-carb pastas, but beware; some of them still have a considerable amount of carbs.

Directions:

Sauce: 24-27 minutes. Add the ground beef to a large pan and cook on medium-high heat for 7 minutes. Break it up and turn the burger every minute or so. Add the mushrooms, garlic, and salt. Cook for an additional 7-10 minutes or until the burger is fully cooked and the mushrooms and onions are slightly caramelized. Add the pasta sauce, olives, seasoning. Turn the heat to low and let simmer for another 10 minutes.

Noodles: "spaghetti - skinny pasta." Fry in pan for 2-3 minutes. Done!

#2. Steak and Egg Scramble

Nutrition facts
Servings per meal: 5
Time to cook: 25 minutes
Calories: 507
Fat: 41 grams (369 calories from fat = 73% of meal)
Protein: 31 grams (124 calories from protein = 24% of meal)
Carbs: 4 grams (16 calories from carbs = 3% of meal)

Ingredients:

16 ounces diced steak
6 large eggs
2 cups tomatoes
4 ounces cheddar cheese, sliced or chopped for easy melting
2 cups mushrooms, sliced
2 tablespoons olive oil
¼ cup butter
1 tablespoon Italian seasoning
1 teaspoon salt

Directions:

Fry the steak in a large pan on medium-high heat with olive oil, salt, and Italian seasoning. After 10 minutes of cooking, add the mushrooms and cook for another 5 minutes. Add eggs and butter, stirring occasionally. When eggs are nearly done (after about 7 minutes), add the tomatoes and cheese. Cook until the cheese starts to melt, about 3 minutes. All done! Serve with sour cream if you want to add fat.

#3. Keto Creamy Chicken Fettuccine Alfredo

Nutrition facts
Servings per meal: 5
Time to cook: 30-40 minutes
Calories: 584
Fat: 4.6 grams (437 calories from fat = 75% of meal)
Protein: 31 grams (124 calories from protein = 21% of meal)
Carbs: 8.6 grams (34 calories from carbs = 5% of meal)

Ingredients:

Boneless skinless chicken thighs, qty 5
1 tablespoons minced garlic
1 cup mushrooms, sliced
2 cups chicken broth
1 tablespoon salt
¼ cup butter
1 ½ cups heavy cream
3 packages low-carb pasta "spaghetti - skinny pasta"
1 cup freshly grated parmesan cheese
3 cups chopped broccoli

Directions:

Sauce: Cook chicken thighs in a large pot over medium-high heat. Sprinkle salt on top. Cook chicken on medium-high heat for 10 minutes, keep covered. Flip thighs and cook for 12 more minutes, keep covered. Add chicken broth, butter, cream, broccoli, mushrooms, and garlic. Cook for 18 more minutes, keep covered. Remove lid and add cheese about 5 minutes before its done, stirring occasionally, until it is completely melted. Remove from heat.

Noodles: "Spaghetti - skinny pasta." Fry in pan for 5 minutes with a little butter, turning frequently. Done! Pour sauce over the noodles, add a chicken thigh or 2, and you have a tasty, high-fat, low-carb meal!

#4. "Fat-bomb" Chocolate Peanut Butter Cups

Nutrition facts
Servings: 12
Time to prepare: 10-15 minutes
Calories: 247
Fat: 25 grams (225 calories from fat = 91% of meal)
Protein: 2.4 grams (10 calories from protein = 4.5% of meal)
Carbs: 2.6 grams (10 calories from carbs = 4.5% of meal)

Ingredients:

1 cup coconut oil
½ cup natural peanut butter
2 tablespoons heavy cream
1 tablespoon cocoa powder
1 teaspoon liquid stevia
¼ teaspoon vanilla extract
¼ teaspoon kosher salt
1 package cupcake liners

Instructions:

Put the peanut butter in a saucepan and heat it up until you can pour it into the cupcake liners. Place the rest of the ingredients in another saucepan, put on low heat, and stir until smooth. Put 1-2 teaspoons of peanut butter in each liner and top off with 1-2 teaspoons of the chocolate mixture. Makes 12 chocolate peanut butter cups. Refrigerate or freeze until hard. All Done! Enjoy!

2.6 grams of carbs per peanut butter cup, but I will skimp on carbs all day long to enjoy a couple of these at night!

Shopping List

Broccoli, chopped, 3 cups
Butter, ½ cup
Cheddar cheese, shredded, 4 ounces
Chicken broth, 2 cups
Chicken thighs, Boneless skinless, qty 5 pieces
Cocoa powder, 1 tablespoon
Coconut oil, 1 cup
Cupcake liners, 1 package
Diced steak, 16 ounces
Eggs, 6 large
Garlic, 1 head
Ground beef, 80% (20% fat), organic grass-fed, 1 pound
Heavy cream, 2 cups
Hunts garlic and herb pasta sauce, 1 can (24 oz)
Italian seasoning, 3 tablespoons
Low-carb pasta "spaghetti - skinny pasta" (konjac/shirataki noodles), 5 packages (or 9 servings total)
Mushrooms, sliced, 4 ½ cups
Olive oil, 2 tablespoons
Olives, sliced, 1 small can
Parmesan cheese, freshly grated, 1 ¼ cups
Peanut butter, smooth, ½ cup
Salt, small bottle or 4 tablespoons
Stevia, liquid or powdered, 1 teaspoon
Tomatoes, 3 cups chopped
Vanilla extract, ¼ teaspoon

Part 4
Keto Success

You may find greater success using a specific approach.

All keto diets are high in fat, moderate in protein, and low in carbs. Here are several varieties of commonly practiced keto:

Keto Paleo (Caveman Diet): This diet is based on the types of foods that our ancestors consumed. It consists chiefly of meat, fish, vegetables, and fruit, and excludes grains and most dairy products and processed food.

Ketogenic Mediterranean Diet: Lots of fruits, vegetables, whole grains, legumes, and olive oil. Fish and poultry are preferred over red meat. A little red wine every day.

Keto Vegetarian: There are several types of vegetarians. This diet typically includes all plant foods. Some vegetarians consume dairy products, eggs, fish, and other seafood.

Keto Vegan: Eat anything … except for animal-based foods OF ANY KIND.

Keto, Raw Food: This diet includes only uncooked, plant-based foods.

All these diets (paleo, vegetarian, vegan, and raw food) have been shown to provide substantial health benefits, ESPECIALLY compared to the "SAD" diet (Standard American Diet).

"SAD" diet (Standard American Diet): The diet of the average American: excess sugar, lots of processed foods, food additives, artificial ingredients, and many foods known to be carcinogenic. Limited amounts of healthy fruits, vegetables, and whole foods. Many food addictions are associated with the SAD diet. Food addictions are a real thing. Many people overeat because of the happiness food brings them. However, these good feelings wear off quickly.

Tips for eating keto:

-Processed foods have been shown to have less nutritional value than whole foods.
-Some foods lose nutritional value when they are canned, cooked, or frozen.
-Eat high-quality fats – no trans fats. Always buy organic, with no hormones or antibiotics.

-Eat plenty of vegetables, berries, and nuts.
-Drink adequate amounts of water and electrolytes.
-Listen to your body.
-Consult your doctor for all things related to your health.

-Test for ketones in your urine. (Drinking too much water can affect your results.)
-Nutritional ketosis typically happens within one to four days.
-Don't overeat.
-Keep track of your macros with an app on your phone or computer.
-Having trouble getting into NK? Consider fasting.

Final Words

Nearly every day, scientists and researchers are finding more benefits of the keto lifestyle. Society has brainwashed us to think that fats, in general, are unhealthy. However, as more research comes out, we are finding that the opposite is true. If you are having trouble with your diet, reach out to someone for help. Try not to eat out; also, buy only foods that are acceptable for your regimen. Remove everything from your cupboards and fridge that might tempt you. Take it slow, and you will have fewer difficulties transitioning into your new diet. Continue learning about the foods you've been eating, and try new ones. You may find that you enjoy foods you hated in the past.

This book was written for the sole purpose of helping people transition to the keto lifestyle. If you enjoyed this book, please leave a review on Amazon. This helps promote the cause.

Thank you for reading and good luck with your success!

Derek Shawn

Works cited

Allen, Bryan G. et al. 2014. *Ketogenic Diets as an Adjuvant Cancer Therapy: History and Potential Mechanism.* Redox Biology 2 PMC.

Austin, Gregory L. et al. 2009. *A Very Low-Carbohydrate Diet Improves Symptoms and Quality of Life in Diarrhea-Predominant Irritable Bowel Syndrome.* Clinical gastroenterology and hepatology : the official clinical practice journal of the American Gastroenterological Association

Best TH, et al. 2000. *Cardiac complications in pediatric patients on the ketogenic diet.* Neurology. PubMed.

Bostock, Emmanuelle C. S., Kenneth C. Kirkby, and Bruce V. M. Taylor. 2017. *The Current Status of the Ketogenic Diet in Psychiatry.* Frontiers in Psychiatry 8. PMC.

Brownlow, Milene L. et al. 2017. *Nutritional Ketosis Affects Metabolism and Behavior in Sprague-Dawley Rats in Both Control and Chronic Stress Environments.* Frontiers in Molecular Neuroscience .

C.C., Jordanes. Mierow. 2012. *In: The Origin and Deeds of the Goths.* Princeton, NJ, USA: Princeton University Press.

Dashti HM1, Mathew TC, Hussein T, Asfar SK, Behbahani A, Khoursheed MA, Al-Sayer HM,

Bo-Abbas YY, Al-Zaid NS. 2004. *Long-term effects of a ketogenic diet in obese patients.* Pubmed.

Di Lorenzo, Cherubino et al. 2018. *Efficacy of Modified Atkins Ketogenic Diet in Chronic Cluster Headache: An Open-Label, Single-Arm, Clinical Trial.* Frontiers in Neurology 9. PMC.

Ford ES, Li C, Zhao G. 2010. *Prevalence and correlates of metabolic syndrome based on a harmonious definition among adults in the US.* Journal of Diabetes.

Freeman JM, Kossoff EH, Hartman AL. 2007. *The ketogenic diet: one decade later.* Pediatrics PMID.

Gynecologists, American College of Obstetricians and. 2015. *Polycystic ovary syndrome.* http://www.acog.org/Patients/FAQs/Polycystic-Ovary-Syndrome-PCOS.

Jason D. Michaels M.D., M.S., et al. 2015. *Case Report of the Keto Rash in the journal: Pediatric Dermatology.* Pediatric Dermatology journal.

Katherine M. Flegal, PhD, Margaret D Carroll, MSPH. 2010. *Prevalence and trends in obesity among adults, 1999-2008.* JAMA.

Kosinski, Christophe, and François R. Jornayvaz. 2017. *Effects of Ketogenic Diets on Cardiovascular Risk Factors: Evidence from Animal and Human Studies.* PMC.

Kossoff EH, Zupec-Kania BA, Rho JM. 2009. *Ketogenic diets: an update for child neurologists.* J Child Neurol.

Martin K, Jackson CF, Levy RG, Cooper PN. 2016. *Ketogenic diet and other dietary treatments for epilepsy.* Cochrane Database Syst Rev.

Masino, Susan A., and David N. Ruskin. 2013. *Ketogenic Diets and Pain.* Journal of child neurology.

Mavropoulos, John C et al. 2005. *The Effects of a Low-Carbohydrate, Ketogenic Diet on the Polycystic Ovary Syndrome: A Pilot Study.* Nutrition & Metabolism 2 .

Meidenbauer JJ, Ta N, Seyfried TN. 2014. *Influence of a ketogenic diet, fish-oil, and calorie restriction on plasma metabolites and lipids in C57BL/6J mice.* . Nutrition & Metabolism. PMC.

other. 2017. *About Polycystic Ovary Syndrome (PCOS) .* https://www.nichd.nih.gov/health/topics/pcos/con ditioninfo.

Pérez-Guisado J1, Muñoz-Serrano A. 2011. *A pilot study of the Spanish Ketogenic Mediterranean Diet: an effective therapy for the metabolic syndrome.* PubMed.

Pi-Sunyer, Xavier. 2009. *The Medical Risks of Obesity.* PMC.

Staff, Mayo Clinic. 2017. *Low-carb diet: Can it help you lose weight?* www.mayoclinic.org/healthy-lifestyle/weight-loss/in-depth/low-carb-diet.

Volek J.S., Phinney S.D., Forsythe C.E., Quann E.E.,
     Wood R.J., Puglisi M.J., Kraemer W.J., Bibus
     D.M., Fernandez M.L., Feinman R.D. 2009.
     *Carbohydrate restriction has a more favorable
     impact on the metabolic syndrome than a low fat
     diet. Lipids.* PubMed, CrossRef.

Yancy, William S et al. 2005. *A Low-Carbohydrate,
     Ketogenic Diet to Treat Type 2 Diabetes.* PMC.

www.ingramcontent.com/pod-product-compliance
Lightning Source LLC
Chambersburg PA
CBHW051400250726
48656CB00006B/2200